HOW I GET AROUND

# AIRPLANES

RYAN EARLEY

## TABLE OF CONTENTS



A Pelican Book

SEAHORSE PUBLISHING

# Teaching Tips for Caregivers and Teachers:

Research shows that one of the best ways for students to learn a new topic is to read about it.

## Before Reading

- Read the title and predict what the book will be about.
- Read the "Words to Know" and discuss the meaning of each word.
- Read the back cover to see what the book is about.

## During Reading

- When a student gets to a word that is unknown, ask them to look at the rest of the sentence to find clues to help with the meaning of the unknown word.
- Motivate students with praise and encouragement.

## After Reading

- Discuss the main idea of the book.
- Ask students to give one detail that they learned in the book.

# Sight Words

a
all
an
around
by
fly
get
have
I
in
the

# Words to Know

airplane

cockpit

engine

landing gear

sky

wings

I get around by **airplane**.

airplane

All airplanes
have **wings**.

wing

engine

All airplanes
have an **engine**.

cockpit

All airplanes have a **cockpit**.

All airplanes fly in the **sky**.

sky

All airplanes have
**landing gear**.

landing gear

# Index



Written by: Ryan Earley
Design by: Niko Magaro
Editor: Kim Thompson
Series Development: James Earley

Photos: All images from Shutterstock

**Library of Congress PCN Data**
Airplanes / Ryan Earley
How I Get Around
ISBN 979-8-8945-9264-0(hard cover)
ISBN 979-8-8945-9278-7(paperback)
ISBN 979-8-8945-9306-7(EPUB)
ISBN 979-8-8945-9292-3(eBook)
ISBN 979-8-8945-9320-3(audio)
ISBN 979-8-8945-9334-0(Read-Along)
Library of Congress Control Number: 2024946367

Printed in Canada/012025/CP20250101

**Seahorse Publishing Company**
seahorsepub.com



**Published in the United States**
**Seahorse Publishing**
PO Box 771325
Coral Springs, FL 33077

SEAHORSE PUBLISHING